A long time ago, when I was just a little boy of maybe six or seven, I didn't like going to school.

One day, my teacher, Nandlal Jharia, called me after all the other students were gone.

He took me to the veranda and drew a dot on the white wall. Yes, a dot.

He said, "Don't feel scared. Just look at this bindu."

# My autobiography for all young painters!

**Our Mission:** Every child reading well and for fun!

I Love Reading Library is a unique series of books that brings new/diffident readers into sustainable learning. With high-quality content and design to match the learning needs of children at different reading levels, it brings the best of India's 2000 years of literary heritage, from the classical to the contemporary—for shared and guided reading. The books help increase young readers' ability to understand BIG Ideas for change; and how to put them to work to break gender and other stereotypes. They help children build a kinder, more sustainable world.

SAYED HAIDER
# RAZA

by

SAYED HAIDER
# RAZA

## ФKATHA

He went inside. I sat there, staring at the dot. When he came back, he patted my back and said, "Shabash, beta. Well done!"

For me, that was the beginning. I started to fix my mind on my studies. He knew I liked to play. He brought play into my lessons.

I started enjoying reading and learning. I became one of his good students.

But I was most interested in nature.

We lived in a small village called Babaria in Mandla district of Madhya Pradesh. My father was a Forest Officer. I saw the river Narmadaji every day from my house.

It was lovely! I saw water, earth, wind and sky.

All inside a square frame.

Our village had many mountains and hills. And many many trees – imli, mango, jamun! We lived among the Gond adivasis and I felt one of them. Their music and dance was the only sound that we heard in the silent forest.

There were many animals and birds in the forest. Sometimes even a tiger came to our village!

I wanted to put the nature I saw onto a piece of paper in pencil or in colour. I wanted to learn art!

My father sent me to Nagpur for art studies.

And after two years in Nagpur, I went to Sir J. J. School of Art in Bombay.

There were so many painters in Bombay! Together we started asking many questions about art.

We talked a lot. We discussed a lot. We argued a lot. We were always working. Even while sleeping, we were working!

My nine years in Bombay were my most fascinating years!

About fifty-sixty years ago, Paris was the only place to love for modern artists from all over the world.

After World War II, many Indian artists travelled to Paris to soak in all they could of the art it offered.

I was lucky to be one of them!

I was learning a new visual language. But at the heart of it was always nature. Prakriti.

It was the fire and water, earth, wind and sky, brought together within a geometric framework.

For me, they were all of nature and our lives coming together!

The idea of nature was very important in my childhood. But in Bombay I realized that a painter should know the language of art as a writer should know the language of words.

A writer must have mastery over words and grammar when writing. And a painter should know what colour is.

Within my visual language, I discovered the bindu. It is much more than a dot.

To me, bindu is the centre, a source of energy. It is the beginning and the end ... The same bindu that my teacher had drawn on the white wall of the veranda of my school when I was just a little boy, a long time ago.

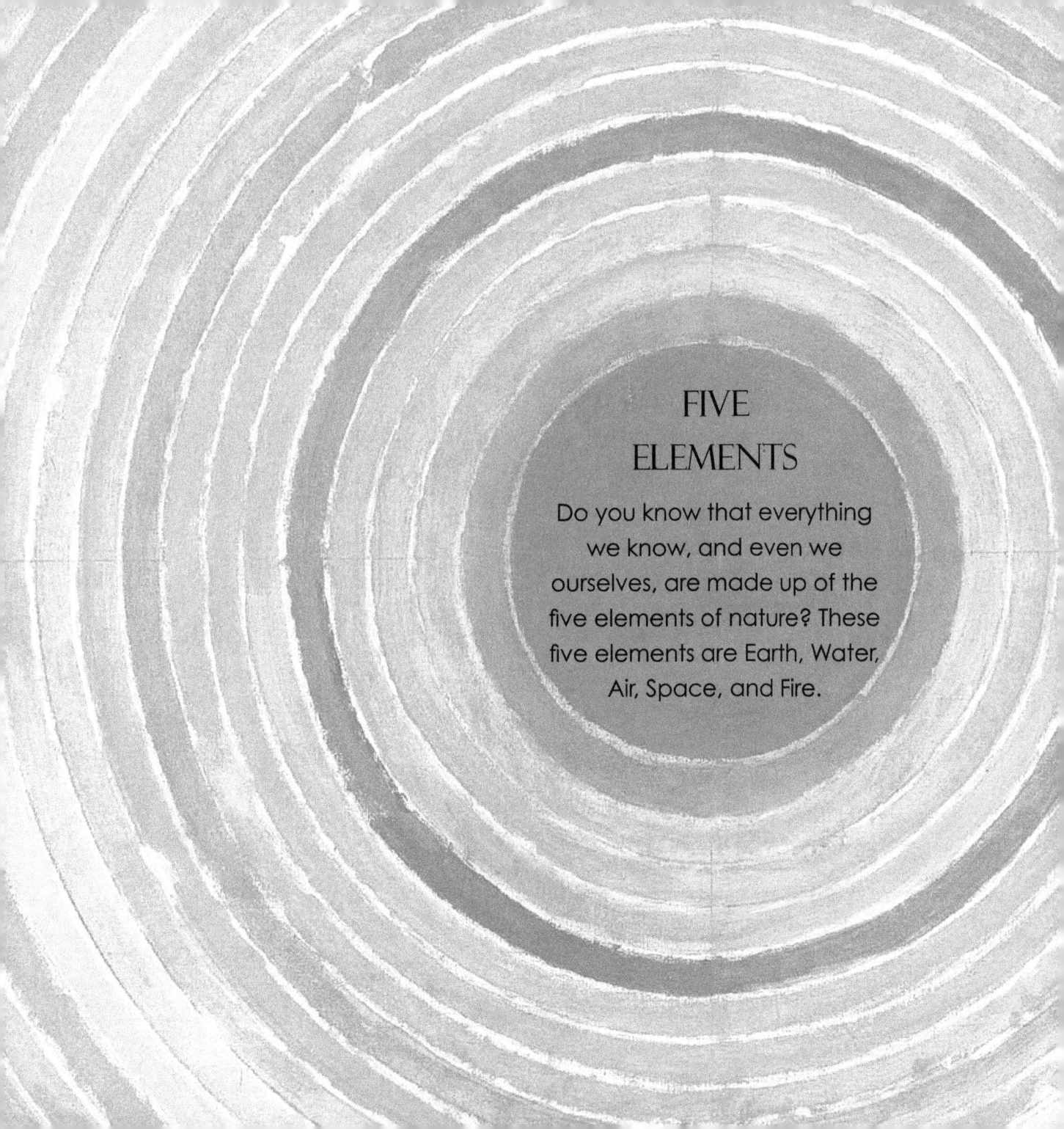

# FIVE ELEMENTS

Do you know that everything we know, and even we ourselves, are made up of the five elements of nature? These five elements are Earth, Water, Air, Space, and Fire.

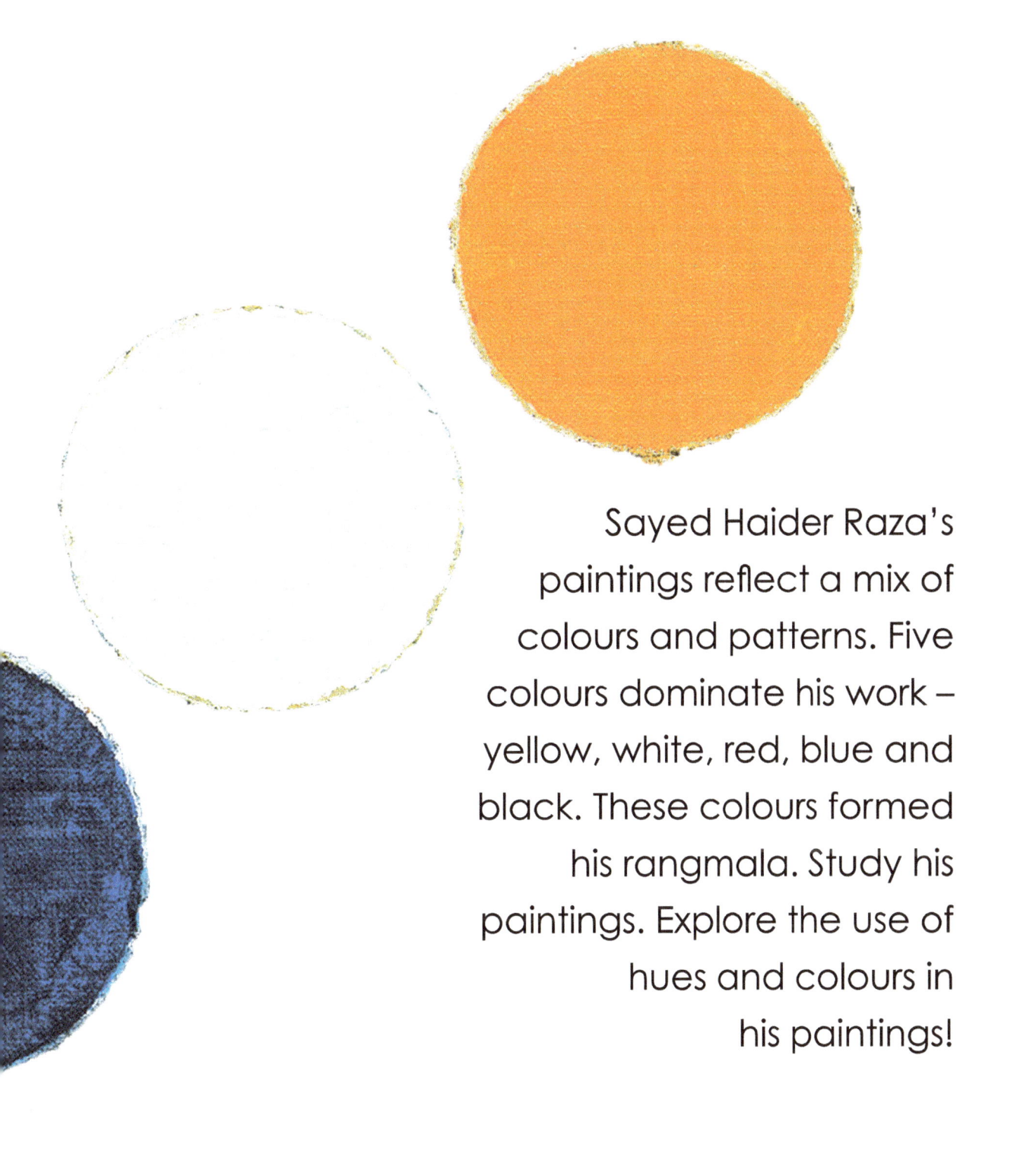

Sayed Haider Raza's paintings reflect a mix of colours and patterns. Five colours dominate his work – yellow, white, red, blue and black. These colours formed his rangmala. Study his paintings. Explore the use of hues and colours in his paintings!

# DISCOVER THE ARTIST WITHIN YOU!

## ACT

Scientists say that artists have a brain that is different. Their brain helps them to day dream, to imagine, to create stuff that no one has thought of!

Want an artist's brain? Come, train your brain to be an artist's brain!

## BE CURIOUS

Imagine you are Raza. Now, think of your favourite geometric shape — a square, a circle, or a triangle! Draw using your favourite shape.

Remember: Artists are curious people!

## India is a very colourful country.

### DREAM AWAY

What is your favourite dream? Do your dreams make you afraid, or make you laugh? Artists are sometimes inspired by their dreams.

Try and remember a dream that you had recently. Now try to capture it in a drawing.

## THINK BIG IDEAS

How do artists come up with unusual ideas? Discuss with your friends ways to get crazy ideas for paintings! Even a shadow can set your mind thinking!

Maintain a diary. Draw something every day.

Change the world into something that is specially yours. Like Raza!

## DO VISUAL PUSH-UPS EVERY DAY

Show your love for colour in your art!

# GUESS!

Look at the paintings below. Match each painting to the page of this book on which it appeared first!

Om, 2013

Pradesh, 2014

Kundalini, 2013

Rangraag, 2013

Aarakt Shyam, 2012

Purush Prakriti, 2013

Bindu Panch Tatva, 2014

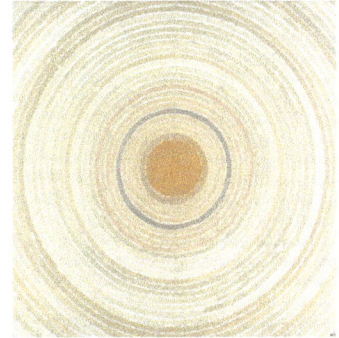
Shanti Bindu, 2006

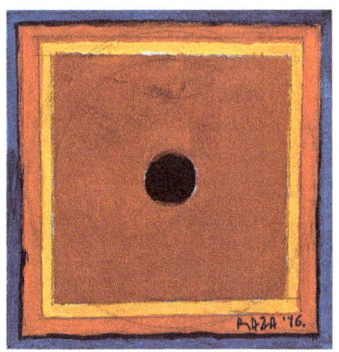
Vatayan, 2016

Panch Tatva, 2002

Haut de Cagnes, 1951

Aarambh, 2014

Untitled, 1948

Detail, Rangraag, 2013

# RAZA, THE MAN WHO LOVED COLOURS!

Sayed Haider Raza was born on 22 February 1922. He started painting when he was twelve. He continued painting almost till the day he died, on 23 July 2016, at the age of 94!

Raza lived and worked in Paris for many years. He made many, many paintings, won many, many awards!

Raza Saab was a good painter. But more than that, he was a good human being!

## DO YOU LOVE COLOURS?

If yes, then you can be a Raza too!
Just keep painting every day. Practice to see the world differently!

Set up under the guidance of Mr. Sayed Haider Raza, The Raza Foundation is an organization that works in the areas of art and culture. The Foundation has been instrumental in creating spaces for various art and culture programmes, bringing out publications that reflect India's diverse art, providing fellowships to the younger talent, and also carrying out a deeper research into the works of the great Indian masters.

## क कथा

Katha is a globally recognised non-profit organization (www.katha.org) that has been working in the literacy to literature continuum since 1988. Our nearly 30 years of experience is in publishing and education for children in poverty.

"Katha has a real soft corner for kids. Which is why it … create[s] such gorgeous picture books for children."
— **Time Out**

"Katha stands as an exemplar for all the creative projects around the world that grapple with ordinary and dramatic misery in cities."
— **Charles Landry, The Art of City Making**

### THE 300M CHALLENGE

India has 300 million 4-18 year olds in school today, 50% of them not reading at grade-level. Can we as a nation work together to bring every child to sustained reading?

We in Katha cannot achieve this challenge alone. The 300 Million Alliance is a national network of partners and collaborators, under the leadership of Katha, that runs the national reading alliance, a quick, affordable and ambitious route to reach sustainable reading to India's 300 million children. To know more, do write to us at editors@katha.org.

We thank our awesome partner, The Raza Foundation, for making this book possible.

KATHA

First published by Katha, 2017 | A3, Sarvodaya Enclave, Sri Aurobindo Marg, New Delhi 110 017
Copyright © Katha, 2017 | Phone: 91-11 4141 6600 . 4182 9998 . Fax: 91-11 2651 4373
Text copyright © Katha, 2017 | E-mail: editors@katha.org, Website: www.katha.org
Paintings copyright © The Raza Foundation, 2017

ISBN 978-93-82454-50-2

All rights reserved. No part of this book may be reproduced or utilized in any form without the prior written permission of the publisher.

Ten per cent of sales proceeds from this book will support the quality education of children studying in Katha Schools.
Katha regularly plants trees to replace the wood used in the making of its books.

# Make friends with Katha books!

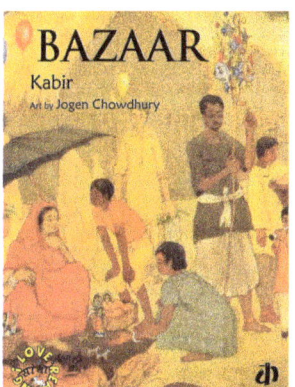

**A Tree | Klara Koettner-Benigni | Art by Tribal and Folk Artists of India**
Life on earth would be impossible without our precious friends – the trees!

**Dear Earth | Avvaiyar | Art by Murali Nagapuzha**
A lyrical tribute to earth's amazing kindness!

**Bazaar | Kabir | Art by Jogen Chowdhury**
Experience the sights, smells and sounds of a bazaar!

**Tigers Forever! | Ruskin Bond | Art by David Stribbling**
Let's protect and save our tiger friends!

**Why? | Michio Mado | Art by Oscar Bluemner**
Can nature ever be old? Find out in this poem!

www.ingramcontent.com/pod-product-compliance
Lightning Source LLC
LaVergne TN
LVHW070059080426
835508LV00028B/3454